I0521926

a lot
like
love

a lot like love

a collection of poems written by

sonia sabnis

CINNAMONTEAL
DESIGN & PUBLISHING

First published in India in 2019 by CinnamonTeal Publishing

Copyright © 2019 Sonia Sabnis

ISBN 978–93–87676–38–1

BISAC Code: POE000000/POETRY/General

Sonia Sabnis asserts the moral right to be identified as the author of this work. All rights reserved. No part of this publication may be produced, stored in a retrieval system, or transmitted in any form or by any means without the prior written permission of the publisher, except by reviewers, who may quote brief passages in a review, nor be otherwise circulated in any form of binding or cover other than that in which it is published and without a similar condition being imposed on the subsequent purchaser.

Book and Cover design: Sonia Sabnis

CinnamonTeal Publishing
an imprint of CinnamonTeal Design and Publishing
Plot No 16, Housing Board Colony
Gogol, Margao
Goa 403601 India

www.cinnamonteal.in

To every person who had faith in me, and in my ability to write this book – *I am grateful for you.* You may have believed in my words, but it were your motivating words that made me believe I could do this. On days, when I almost gave up, your encouraging voice guided me to keep going. For that, I thank you.

From the bottom of my heart, *thank you.*

To the ones trapped in a toxic relationship-

Do not let the fear of being alone
or the possibility of not finding love again,
keep you in a relationship
where you already feel alone
and where you aren't being loved right.
You deserve the absolute best, and nothing less.
Don't ever forget that.

Chapter 1

First comes the
ILLUSION

In the same way
that flowers fall from a tree,
with hope,
that before they touch the ground,
the wind will catch them
and transport them
to a beautiful place;
I too fell.
And once I did,
Love came,
caught me in its gentle embrace
and it carried me to the
most beautiful sight in the world.

It carried me to you.

In a crowded room, with loud chatter in the air,
as people laugh and converse and move around,
I look up. I look up, and amidst the fleeting
chaos, I see you looking right back at me. All
of a sudden, everybody else is just colours and
sounds, and in that moment, it's just you and I-
our eyes locked, my heart giddy.

You almost disappeared into the crowd, with the pain of the weight you carry, masked under a fake laugh. So when I stopped in front of you, you were surprised. You expected me to walk past you, like everyone else did. But I didn't. Instead I reached beyond the façade you created, and picked your heavy suitcase.

'Let me carry the weight for a while,' I said.

And when you looked at me with relief in your eyes, I realised what they meant when they said- sometimes, all it takes, is to be in the right place, at the right time.

There was something about him that captured my attention. Like reading the first three lines of a book, a glimpse into his eyes, was all it took for me to realise, that I needed to know his story.

I stumbled across you
in a dark, crowded hallway.
And although everyone,
except you,
held a bright light,
I chose to walk in your direction.
And I think that's because,
right from the start,
it was your *darkness*
that drew me towards you.

You are a vault- with codes that nobody can decrypt and chains that nobody can break. *You are so guarded*, that the world remains unaware of what really lies within you. And I, with my lust for cryptic things, cannot seem to turn away from you. So I decide- no matter how guarded you are with the rest of the world, I will have you trust me enough, to let me inside.

At the centre
of all the chaos
you stood,
with no fear,
and only wonder in your eyes.
I was awestruck.
I wanted to know
what made you
look at destruction,
and see beauty
hidden somewhere.
And the longer
I looked at you,
the sooner
I answered my own question.

As you sat in front of me- a cigarette delicately caught between your fingers- and spoke of every woman who had taken a jab at your heart, I leaned forward and listened eagerly. And right then, I knew. I knew, that although I wasn't smoking, in that moment, I was addicted to something far more intoxicating.

You.

I didn't believe
in *perfection*
until I saw you-
freckles marking constellations
on your cheeks
as you stood in the sunlight,
wearing your flaws
on your sleeve,
laughing with everyone
because you wore
your shirt inside out.

My pulse beats through my veins
at a great speed,
while my eyes play dodge with yours.
My insides- they become home
to a thousand butterflies,
while my heart, it beats so hard,
that I imagine it leaping out.
My body turns into a waterfall-
a cascade of overflowing emotions.
And my legs feel,
like rubber sometimes,
and other times, like stone.
I am as disorganised as laundry
on a Sunday morning,
and the only explanation I have for it is this-

I have been invaded by love.

Love, they say,
is complicated.
But as he stood
in my balcony at 3 am,
breathless and covered in dirt,
after climbing the pipe
that led to my house,
I was certain
that they were wrong.
Love was as simple
as looking at someone
and feeling every emotion,
all at once.

The moment I laid my eyes on you, I felt a tremor. At first, I thought, how beautiful it was that the Earth shook a little to mark this magical moment for us. But after a while I realised that it wasn't a tremor I had felt. You see, it was my anxious heart. It shook turbulently, because it knew, that from the moment I laid my eyes on you, *it had been compromised.*

At some point in our life, we all wish for someone to belong to us. Someone who will return to us, every night, no matter what. So we spend our time, turning ourselves into homes- homes where people can collapse at the end of a tough day. Homes, where people can find love, when everything else in the world offers them pain. We do this, and we wait. We wait for someone to come into our life, take a look around and decide, that this is where they want to stay.

Love, I realised, was something that existed in me. Whether it was alive or dead, depended on the people I was around. Most men couldn't trigger butterflies in my stomach, which meant that the Love in me, was lying unconscious. But around you, my heart shrieks like a red light on an ambulance, and I feel alive. You give life to the love in me, and I am addicted to how liberating that feels. So I hand my body over to you, in hope that the chemical explosions I feel every time you look me in the eye, never stop.

There is an echo amongst the trees
as the birds chirp incandescently.
The wind feeds laughter to the day,
and the sun beams brightly
from its faraway throne.
There is an unknown happiness in the air.
I can feel it in every breath I take.
There is music among the greens
and a blushing whisper
amidst the blue skies.
Tell me,
is this what it feels like?

Does love add life to every little thing?

You sit in front of me,
your lips moving in conversation,
while I watch you star struck.
To me, you are like a constellation
fallen out of the sky-
gorgeous and unreal.
So I pinch my arm
under the table,
to make sure this is real.
And it is.
I am here.
You are here.
And we're drinking coffee together,
blushing pink smiles
and pouring secrets onto the table,
silently wishing,
that our time together
never runs out.

You list your insecurities
and name all your flaws;
and that only makes me feel
like I have magic in my bones.
Magic, that lets me see
what you don't.
Because when I look at you,
oh when I look at you,
all I see is *breath-taking beauty*.

I woke up one morning and everything was different. My mind was flooded with only one thought- well, numerous thoughts about one, single person- *you*. And as I went about my day, every small incident that happened, from the paper cut I got while reading to the car I almost hit while driving- I wanted to tell you about it all. And even when my mind was meant to be occupied by other things, my thoughts somehow drifted back to you. I missed you in a way I had never missed anyone.

Is this what happens when you're in love?
Does your heart grow restless in his absence?
Does it ache for him, desperately,
the way lungs crave air?

I fell in love
with the way
he looked at the world-
with complete wonder
and star struck eyes.
As if he were a boy,
sitting in the audience,
watching a circus act
and everything around him
was *pure magic*.

Sometimes when I am looking at you, I allow my eyes to linger for a little longer than usual. I do so, because I want to remember everything about you. Your shy eyes. Your pink lips. Your freckled nose. Your captivating smile. And so I allow my eyes to linger. I look at you for as long as it takes my mind, to find within itself, an eternal place to store you.

Do you know that feeling? When you're looking at him and he's the only one in focus, while the rest of the crowd is blur? When time slows down and his eyes look perfectly brown, and there's a certain glow to his smile that makes your heart skip and jump? *Do you know that feeling?* The same heavy feeling you get when you reach the top of a Ferris wheel. And just before you make the drop, your eyes are stuck. You cannot seem to look away, because deep down you know. You know that in this moment, there is no better view than this.

After talking on the phone for hours,
narrating excerpts from our day to each other,
you say goodnight and hang up.
Even after the line gets cut,
I stand still, staring at my phone,
with a smile on my face.
I realise then,
that there has been
a shift in the universe.
You are now the sun to me,
and that ball of flaming fire in the air,
is just another star.

I had heard of love before, but never felt it. I had watched it in movies and read about it in books- and all of it told me only one thing. Being in love meant being happy. And you make me happy. You make me forget about every one of my problems and in your presence, I can feel my heart laughing constantly. So if this feeling of -walking in the sunshine, with a skip in my step, thinking of you from morning to night, wishing the day had more hours so that I could spend it all with you- means love, then yes,

I am, hopelessly and undeniably, in love.

There is an ongoing race between everyone- each of us losing breathe, chasing after love. And so, in that beautiful moment when someone confesses their love for you, your heart feels like it's going to explode with happiness. You feel relieved, because it's like you finally crossed the finish line and you won. Now, it's your chance to collapse, peacefully, in the arms of love.

I have a photograph of you. And every time I look at it, I think of exactly what happened before and after I clicked that photograph. Before, you were sitting in front of me telling me stories of your childhood: the pranks you played, the wounds you felt, the bittersweet memories you made. And somewhere in the middle, you stopped and stared into nothingness. That was when I clicked that photograph of you. As you travelled back in time. And after? After I captured your smile, after I heard you talk about the stories that made you, you,

I fell in love.

I want to keep you safe. In my arms, away from the pain, I want to keep you safe. Sometimes, I fear the line I am willing to cross to keep you happy. There is no rulebook in my mind, when it comes to you- there is nothing that can tell me what is wrong and what is right. I simply follow the footsteps of my heart to wherever it wants to take me, because I would do anything, absolutely anything, to keep you happy.

Your charming eyes.
Your dimpled smile.
These are things
that make poetry.
And I,
the one they call a poet,
am actually not.
I am simply an admirer,
who adds ink to paper,
while you-
you sit there
existing
and exhaling poetry,
all in the same breath.

You are
the endless road,
and I am
the white line
that runs with it.
I begin
where you begin,
and I end
where you end.

You make me want to talk about all the things I never say out loud, he said. And I melted like ice to his warm words. He made me feel special-like I was the only one who actually knew him; like I alone had the power to undress his cloak of secrets.

You wrap your hands
around my waist,
and pull me
as close to your chest
as our bodies allow.
In the silence of the night,
our hearts align,
with just two layers of flesh
keeping them apart.
And for a moment, just then,
I swear, I could feel
our hearts beating together
in *perfect harmony*.

I was never afraid of drowning, but that was until I realised that water wasn't the only thing that could drown you. His eyes, they drew me in, so powerfully, that I was transfixed. I couldn't look away. He was like that part of the ocean people avoided, because it was too dangerous. And despite knowing that, I let him lure me in. Under the spell of his beautiful brown eyes, I followed him to the deep end of the ocean and it was only when I looked up, that I realised- the sky was closing in on me and I was, in fact, *drowning*.

I have fallen in love with you.

The kind of love you don't fall out of.

I gave myself to you. All of me. My mind, my heart, my body, my soul. I handed it all over to you. And from the moment you caught them in the palm of your hand, I knew that these were things I would never get back. They all belonged to you now.

I, belonged to you now.

I play you like a movie in my mind and press pause, enough times, to memorize every detail about you. And most nights, the same moments take over me. I relive your laughter and I rethink our conversations, until my mind eventually blocks out everything else. It knows of you and nothing but you; and I realise then, how lethal love can be. For I have given you control over not just my heart, but over every corner of my mind, too.

It all happened so fast. Love caught me by the shoulders and engulfed me. Before I knew it, it was running through my system, making its way to my heart. I felt warm- like someone had lit a fire in the cold parts of my body. *It all happened so fast*, that I couldn't tell whether it was you, I fell in love with, or that sweet feeling of warmth.

Chapter 2

Then comes
CLARITY

I sat on the shore and told the ocean all about you. I spoke of how much I loved you, and how little you loved me. *Your secret is safe with me*, the ocean whispered, and then the blue waves swallowed my love story. I sat there, while it sank to the bottom of the ocean, and thought to myself-

A love like ours isn't meant to stay afloat, I guess.

There is a type of love they never warned us about. The type that uses your kindness as bait, to lure you into deeper waters, and then abandons you while you struggle to stay afloat. This is the kind of love I wish they had told me more about, and not the kind that ends with a happily ever after. In reality, love isn't as pink and easy as the fairy tales say they are. I just wish someone had told me that, before I foolishly allowed myself to be drowned in the name of love.

I got lost,
trying to explore
the meaning of love,
and you found me-
clueless and naïve.
You promised to show me
what love meant.
But after you took my heart
and contaminated it
with your impurity,
all I learnt was
the bitter taste of pain,
and not the sweet feeling of love.

He leaned on me, exhausted from all his previous heartbreaks, and I held him, while whispering honeyed hope into his ears. I carried him, that way, for a long time. Conquered by pain, he could hardly walk, and so I let him lean on me for as long as he needed.

And that is the mistake I made. I revealed to him my weakness- my inability to walk away from someone who is in pain. And once he knew that, he used it against me. He held me captive. He kept me in his life, not because he wanted me, but because he needed me. My hands were meant to heal his tormented heart; my presence, was meant to make him feel less lonely.

We all have that one person in our life, who no matter what, we cannot seem to let go of. That one person, who will hurt us, drag us through the dirt and make us jump in front of a bullet for them, only to realise, that they themselves are holding the trigger. Such people, they convince us that they are worth our tears and pain. They are that one unhealthy habit we can't seem to get rid of; they are the ones who talk us into the idea that *love is meant to be this way.*

They tell you
how to get over
an addiction to cigarettes,
alcohol, drugs and other things.
But what about love?
How do I overcome
this desire I have,
to run back into your arms,
knowing, that my love for you
is lethal enough to kill me?

I like to think of myself
as a strong person.
You know,
someone who can say no,
when required to.
But when it comes to you,
I am all of a sudden
caught under a spell.
My armour melts away
and I turn into someone I am not.
You make me weak in my knees
and that scares me.
It scares me,
how easily you can make me feel
as fragile as glass.

They see me jumping through hoops for you and say, that I am blinded by love. But they don't get it. Yes, I run to you every time you call, yes I put aside my own problems to solve yours, yes I give you endless love despite receiving none at all. But what they don't understand, is that I can't help it, because when it comes to you, there strikes a war between my mind and my heart. And unfortunately,

it is a war my mind always loses.

I guess it's the simple idea of being wanted; the idea of being what another person needs. It triumphs over everything else. It seduces our minds so heavily, that we do not look at it from close enough, to check if it is love. We do not care. We like the feeling of being special to someone, and so we give our hearts away to any person who says they love us- *whether they mean it or not.*

Sometimes, everyone around you is aware that the relationship you are in, is not a good one. But you don't listen to what they have to say. You see someone who occasionally gives you his time and effort, who often makes up excuses for his behaviour and who rarely cleans the mess he creates, and you think, *'Oh well, this is all I deserve.'* And so you swallow this poison and trick your body into thinking it is love.

There is nothing more toxic
than a relationship
in which only one person
is in love,
and the other
is simply comfortable.

It's unhealthy for me- the way I love you. I admit, it's unhealthy for me. But I am helpless. My stubborn heart mistakes your toxicity for love and there is not a thing I can do to make it think otherwise.

I think I finally understand what they mean when they *say love is blind*. Sometimes, in a relationship, we ignore all that is in plain sight. We overlook the small mistakes they make. We readily accept every callous apology they throw our way. We never question the manner in which they mistreat us, nor do we acknowledge the fact that the number of times they make us sad, conquers the number of times they make us happy. We get so carried away by the notion of love that we blur the reality before us. And we convince ourselves that with time, things will get better, but the truth is, in a love so toxic, *things are only bound to get worse*.

You own a part of my heart. I use the word 'own' and not 'occupy' because you aren't just another renter. No, you have entered my life and settled here- now you control what my heart does and wants. You have this power over me which makes me want to grant your every wish, without thinking about how exhausting that'll be for me. I am no longer the one who runs my life; you do. I am simply a body- hands tied, mind blind, will lost. And you; you are the captain harbouring this ship into dangerous waters.

I heard your words,
but didn't look
into your eyes
or at your actions,
when you said
you loved me.
And that's where
I went wrong.

You are not entirely responsible for my broken heart. I am a culprit, too. I see your soul, tattered and torn, and I am immediately drawn towards it. This innate need I have, to love and fix anything that is broken- it'll be my destruction. I repeatedly sabotage my own heart, trying to sew together someone else's torn story.

There is a rope tied around my wrist, and its tail end is in your hands. And this rope is very long. It allows me to walk in whichever direction I choose to, but it also allows you, to drag me back whenever you want.

Sometimes, I forget that I carry this weight along with me. I forget for a while, that my life is ultimately controlled by you. But then I feel a small tug at my wrist. And then it all comes back to me. You, my hellish fate, and this insanity you call love.

With you, I seem to be walking in circles. It's like I am living the same heart ache, over and over again, because every time I talk myself into walking away, you somehow convince me to stay. Now, I can no longer tell the difference between what's real and what's not. On some days, you make me feel happy and loved. Other days, you are so cold and harsh towards me, that I question the entire foundation our relationship is built on. My mind, it is lost in this chaos, unable to decide which side of you it should believe. And so I continue walking in circles. I continue living the same heart ache over and over and over again.

I don't know what's worse.
The sound of you leaving
or the sound of your return.

I am exhausted. I am mentally exhausted, waiting for you to make up your mind. Like a wind chime, I stay still, until you, like a wild breeze, come and rattle me up. And just as I turn calm, when you leave, you return once again to unsettle me. This goes on for days and months and now I fear, that this is how my entire life will be. I will spend every day, trying to get over you, and you-

you will swoop in and undo all my effort.

A cup of tea, after staying still for a while, shows bubbles on its surface. These bubbles, they slowly make their way to the walls of the cup, forming a circular layer around it.

I am that cup of tea and the circular layer around me is the wall I am trying to build, to keep you out. But you. You are a silver spoon, stubborn and hell-bent. You stir within me a whirlpool of chaos which breaks down every pillar of strength I built.

A tree will never grow
to its full potential,
if you keep on uprooting it.
I will never bloom
into the person I could be,
until you *set me free*
from your uncertainty.

I am moving on. I am pushing myself every day in a direction that is far away from you. And I am progressing towards a place, where the idea of you doesn't hurt me. But then you do, what you always do. You cut me at my knees. You drag me back to the place where it all began, and I realise, *there's no way I can escape you.*

I feel like I am stuck in a maze, trying to find my way out. I am lost, confused, sad and broken, and on most days I feel like I am repeating the same steps; like I am making absolutely no progress in getting out. And as the days go by, I feel an emptiness settle in my heart. Like I no longer care about escaping this misery.

I am lost in you, and it doesn't matter
how hard I try to get out-
your uncertainty holds me captive;
your love, it misleads me.

You lit a fire in me to warm yourself up. And although you did it for your own interest, it warmed me, too. It made me feel alive. But when you left, you unleashed a storm. For days and days, there was loud thunder and endless rain. And after it passed, I stood under the sky, damp and worn out, trying to helplessly strike a fire in me.

But no matter how hard I tried, *I could not.*

I cannot sleep at night, because as soon as night falls, the monsters come out and pick at my brain. They laugh at me, and they are right to- for how silly I was, to see a trap so beautifully laid, and mistake it for love.

I was falling deeper and deeper into you, and you let that happen, knowing that you wouldn't be able to love me the way I should be loved. You were like the grey ocean. You let the people who swam on your turf, believe, that they had found a home in you. You made them feel safe, and then all of a sudden, you swallowed them whole and spat them out as broken pieces, that would never again dare to love.

Nobody will know of how many nights I spent awake, listening to my heart weep softly. Nobody will know of the endless tears that leak onto my pillow, or the thoughts that torment me till the break of dawn. Nobody will know, including me, why despite such suffocating pain, I return to you loyally. All I know, is that I am chained to you, with a key in my hand, but no courage to leave and let go of your toxic love.

You have never been the kind of person who cancels plans, or says "I am really busy, maybe some other time." You never say *no* to a request or ask favours from people as easily as they ask favours from you. You are the kind of person who never gives up; who never walks away. No, you stay instead. No matter how horrible the relationship is, you stay, because you know how lonely and insecure it feels to be abandoned. You know how much it hurts when someone decides that you aren't worth their time. So you stay, because you are too kind to put someone else through that sort of excruciating pain.

The worst thing about being in a toxic relationship is that you know exactly what is happening. Most people think that you submit yourself to it, blindly, but the truth is, that you know how wrong you are being treated. And you do nothing about it, because by then, your belief in everything, including yourself, vanishes. You feel a kind of numbness- like the part of you that helped you feel emotions, no longer exists. So you allow yourself the torture. You know that it is wrong. You know that it isn't love, but your heart kind of gives up on you, and your mind shuts off, too; so you're left with no cavalry to fight this war.

And so you succumb.

We humans, tell ourselves, that a little pain is justified in love. And I believe that is true, to some extent. Mistakes that hurt both people in a relationship, are usually caused in the spur of the moment and make both partners feel absolutely miserable. This is the pain that is justified in love. But pain that is caused, on purpose, and repeatedly, while aware just how horrible it makes the other person feel, is pain that is not justified in love. We all want to be loved, I know we do, but remember, love comes free. So if you find yourself paying a price to be loved, then walk away, because that isn't how it should be.

Sometimes we wrongfully stumble into relationships that aren't good for us. Relationships that distort our mind, completely, and turn us into someone we're not. We lose our way. We wake up, one day, look around and realise that the life we had, is gone. Instead, we have a new life now; a life driven by the choices of someone else.

And if this has happened to you- if you have stumbled into a toxic relationship, I want you to ask yourself one question: is this person- this person who has distanced you from your own life- worth losing yourself for?

He doesn't ask about you, when you two talk, neither does he listen intently when you open up. He forgets things you already told him and leaves you wondering, more often than not, whether this is really love. But you make excuses for his behaviour and convince yourself that this is something you two can work on.

Now, just take a moment, and contemplate on whether this is what you really want. Do you want to waste your time teaching him how you should be loved? Or do you want to walk away from this relationship, and instead wait for someone who will put in the effort, all by himself, to make you feel utterly loved?

They want you to stay, because you make them feel less lonely. But you do not deserve that. You do not deserve to be in someone's life only to help them overlook the absence of others. You deserve to be fought for. You deserve to be loved compassionately and wholly, and with a fire that will never fail to keep you warm. So don't give yourself away to people who want you, only to fill up the human-sized gap someone else left in them. You are not just a body. You are made up of feelings and emotions, likes and dislikes, a personality and a soul. Be with someone who recognises all of that, and loves you for it.

Not everyone you meet, will love you as deeply as you love them. Some people will simply pull you into their lives, out of boredom, and keep you guessing about what they want from you. They will tell you what you want to hear, when you need it the most, but other times they will treat you like you mean nothing at all. You will not be able to stop yourself from loving such people, but you must. You must will yourself to walk away, because if not, you will spend your entire life wasting your time on someone who values neither you, nor your love.

Chapter 3

PART I

First you
LEAVE

I am tired.
I am tired of always
being the girl
you fall on,
and not once,
the girl you fight for.

For far too long, I stood with an armour of courage, unbeatable by the pain you threw my way. But I no longer can. My strength is crumbling, my will to survive is lost and I am on the verge of collapsing from recurrent heart ache.

I am beginning to understand your game. The way you stroll into my life whenever you want. You reopen every wound, and you pick on every scar. You make me believe the lies I fell for, all over again. And when you leave, I am left to clean the mess you've made. For a long time you have walked in, you have walked out. But I think my heart has decided,

it's time to shut the doors now.

You took too long to make up your mind, about whether you loved me or not. And so now, I have made up mine.

I think it's time I said goodbye.

Once upon a time,
I loved you unconditionally.
I would turn blind to your flaws
and convince myself
that your mistakes
were just a one-time thing.
And that's why you were so shocked
when I chose to leave you.
All that time,
I let you believe that
you could toss me around.
I let you believe that
you could throw a drama,
and I'd sit through it all.
So when I got up midway
and walked out of your little show,
you were surprised to see
that after all this time,
I still had a little bit of fire in me.

Sometimes, I think that maybe
it was all my fault.
I treated you like a rose.
I loved you,
like you were something rare.
And when your crimson red
turned a darker shade,
even then, I loved you
with all my heart.
And I think,
that is why I am at fault.
I saw all the signs:
I saw all your soft petals
turn into something sharp,
yet I chose to believe
that you were the kind of rose
that couldn't have thorns.

I fill the tub, up to its brim, in memories of you. I put my hand into the tub and immediately pull back. The scalding hot memories, they burn me, like salt on a wound. Despite knowing this, I undo my robe and get into the tub. One foot. Second foot. I sit down and then I lay back.

I drown the screaming agony of my burning heart, by simply sinking my body deeper and deeper, into our memories.

I know you miss him. I know you want to crawl back into his arms and stay there. I know your mind keeps rocking back and forth between "You made the right choice," and "Call him, you need him." But baby girl, tell yourself again why you walked away. Remind yourself of the calls he never returned, of the promises he made and broke. Think of the days he didn't show up, think of all the meaningless sorries; think of how he did everything with only half a heart and remind yourself that *that's not really love*.

In a corner of my mind,
I store all the memories
I don't want to remember
and all the things
I don't want to deal with.
I put them in this corner
and soon forget that they exist.
But sometimes,
the walls around these memories
break down
and a few of them appear
in my consciousness.
When this happens, I panic.
I try building the walls back,
but as I do,
more memories start overflowing,
and that's when
everything turns blue,
and I start drowning.

The cuts you left-
they never really stopped bleeding.
And on nights
I spend thinking about you,
they open up and
unearth painful memories
that travel through
my body, like a tremor,
and leave me with a great ache.
I've tried to heal them,
I have, but they stay,
like a souvenir, to remind me,
that I once loved a boy,
who didn't love me back.

I think of it now, and feel that if I were watching my life like a movie in a theatre, I'd yell at my character to run away from that kind of love. The kind of love that pulls you in, keeps you close, but never really fills your heart. The kind that makes you feel like all you are worthy of,

is a bare minimum love.

Today, you woke up thinking of him. You miss him, and that's alright. It's okay to miss someone who was an important part of your life. But there's a reason why he isn't a part of it anymore. He wasn't what you needed. He wasn't the man who would love you the way you deserve to be loved. So don't reach out for the phone, to call him, because that's not a good idea. Your heart it aches for him, I know. But sometimes, you have to deny the heart what it wants and listen to your mind, instead. You have to trust its decision and be strong enough to believe, that you are worthy of a better love.

I know it is scary to walk away from someone who was a constant part of your life. But when that person hurts you intentionally, without caring if you're okay or not, you need to walk away. Learning to live without them will be difficult, but walking away from them is better, than staying with them and being miserable.

You did not deserve the pain he gave you. You did not deserve to be loved half-heartedly. You are beautiful inside-out and I know this, because you chose to love him despite his mistakes. You are forgiving and kind and although he treated you like you meant nothing, you loved him wholly. It takes courage to do that, knowing that they don't love you half as much as you love them. You are stronger than you know, and although you are hurting right now, I know you will fight your way out of this toxic love.

If they beg you to come back, and they will, do not give in to them. Think of why you walked away in the first place. Think of every mistake they made, and every insincere apology they gave you, before repeating their actions all over again. Think of how horrible they made you feel and how insensitive and disrespectful they were towards you. Think of how they hurt you and made you cry, and never once came to console you. If they beg you to come back, and they will, do not give in to them. Think of all the things that drove you away from them, and play them in your mind until you realise that you're better off without them.

Starting over is terrifying. The thought of leaving a relationship that kept you comfortable for so long, and looking for love all over again, is terrifying. But it is important, too. This is when you will get some time with your own self. You will be able to listen to your thoughts more carefully and act towards all the dreams you stashed away before. Starting over can, sometimes, be a good thing, because it gives you the perfect opportunity to leave behind bad choices, and start working towards a better future.

Don't go back to the people who hurt you, deliberately. The ones who knew how horribly they treated you, yet didn't stop. Do not go back to such people, because there is no excuse that could justify their behaviour. You are meant to be cared for- to be loved and nourished, so that you can bloom continuously. You do not deserve to be trampled over, and made to feel like you're not good enough- because you are. You, in all your imperfections, are perfect. So instead of going back to the people who told you that you have no worth, go back to yourself. Return to your inner voice- listen to it when it tells you that you are beautiful, brave and strong.

PART II

Then you
LET GO

They hoisted yellow and blue scarves on rooftops. They covered the water in bowls, with lavender petals, and set candles to float atop them. They played the music of warriors, and dressed in red, all of them, while she sat amidst the chaotic celebration, tears falling onto her scarred hands. The ritual was complete. The girls' virgin heart had been broken by a boy.

Now her strength will finally reveal.

Our strength is an intangible magic that exists somewhere within us. It lies in the dark corners of our bodies and goes unnoticed until we are lost, confused, broken and in need of it. That's when we look inside ourselves. We hunt for it with a desperate hope that only it can save us. And when we finally find it, everything changes. We are no longer afraid of being broken, because what was breakable within us, has already been ripped to pieces and so now, we use this strength to protect whatever is remaining of our damaged heart.

These tears that pool your eyes,
one day, they will stop.
These memories that play in your mind,
one day, they will pause.
The burning pain in your heart,
one day, it will extinguish.
These scars, that every now and then reopen,
one day, they will heal.
Every battle you are fighting right now,
you will eventually conquer.
Remember, time will take
every one of your pains,
and help you turn them into your power.

I hold onto the ends of my sweater, tightly, as I walk down the street. Before the eyes of the world, I feel naked, knowing that beneath this clothing, my body is covered in scars. I look at objects and things, but not at people. I don't look at people, because if anyone would look into my eyes for too long, they'd know that I am made up of *less skin and more scars*.

Sometimes, the chaos in our minds is such, that only we are aware of what's happening within. And we find it difficult to explain something so complicated to someone else. So we don't. Instead we float aimlessly in the sea of our chaos. We let the waves carry us away from every person we were close to.

I don't think twice before being reckless in love anymore. I mean, what's the worst that could happen? I could get hurt? But here's the thing: I have already experienced my share of pain. I've lived with a rock on my chest for years now; so anything after that has just felt like a speck of dust compared to it. So I guess, I am okay with being hurt. I mean, pain doesn't feel so painful, now that I have lived and survived your hurricane.

I started out with a whole heart. And over the years, the men I met, changed that. Every man who walked out on me, left me with a bleeding wound. And soon my heart was a tattered, blood stained cloth covered in the betrayal of men who said they loved me, but didn't. It was unhealthy for me, to keep something so filthy in my body. So I threw it out. I took whatever was left of my heart and threw it out. And now, there is an emptiness in the space it occupied before. ~~I don't love like I did before.~~ *I cannot* love like I did before. And in a way, I believe that's good. My heart was a liability. By ridding myself of it, I have reduced the chances of pain entering my body. After all, they can't hurt what doesn't exist, right?

Today has been a tough day, and it's okay to let weakness grab a hold of you. It's okay to shrink into a corner and cry every tear that you've held back. Your strength- it has powered you for as long as it could- so give it a rest. Let your bones be vulnerable, tonight. Take off the weight you have been carrying for so long, and let your heart mourn the Love that left.

Every line that you draw,
will always come to an end.
Basically, every start has a finish
which means that this pain,
however overpowering
and consuming,
will one day cease to exist.

I know it hurts right now. I know dark rooms and silence is all you want right now. I know thinking of him is too painful, and the questions that knock on your mind, are too loud, to ever let you sleep. But a day will come when he will be lost in the dry tears that cover your pillow. A day will come when his name will sound like a song you played on repeat too many times, and now you're sick of it. A day will come when, from the moment you wake up, you will know that the ache he caused you, is over, and there on he'll be *just another memory*.

Getting over a broken heart isn't easy. It is something that requires commitment. Your mind, it is a vessel of infinite memories, which play on repeat till you tire out. It is your job to distract yourself, as much as you can, and keep your mind from being idle, so that it can't overthink. You need to be strong and refuse your body from wanting him. There is a reason you left him, and that reason should echo loudly in your mind, till you lose all desire to want to return to him.

These wounds you carry in your heart, I know they're heavy. And I wish I could tell you that it will all be okay. But for the next few months, you will suffer. Memories, songs, and places- everything will remind you of him. It will feel like someone is rubbing salt on your wounds. But you've got to endure it all and make it to that place, where the idea of him won't hurt you so much. You've got to carry the weight of this pain, until your heart is strong enough, to leave him behind and move on.

There comes a moment, after the tears have run out, when you're sitting on the floor, trying to accept the fact that your heart is now broken. And in this moment, you have to make a choice. You have to choose between staying amidst the mess of tissues and open wounds, and cleaning them up. You have to choose between grieving over how unfortunate your life is and playing the hand you have been dealt. You have to choose between letting this pain pull you down and letting this pain help you rise stronger.

So tell me, what choice will you make?

Every person
who hurt you,
left you or
chose someone else over you
was a grey cloud.
And while grey clouds
bring despair into your life,
they also eventually make space
for the sun to shine through.
So hold on to hope;
and know, that one day,
the sun rays will find you.

I do not believe that this pain will ever leave me. It will stay, and under its heavy weight, I will transform into someone who will recognise the difference between what love is, and what love is not. I will carry the knowledge of loss and heartbreak in my new bones; I will carry with me the fear of trusting anyone's promises and words.

I do not believe that this pain will ever leave me. But, I do believe that it'll keep me from getting hurt, like I did before, and that one day- one day, I will look back and be grateful for being hurt this way.

Getting your heart broken is like a tradition. It is a ritual every individual needs to experience, in order to know how to survive in this world. Life is filled with paths lain with shards of glass, that'll hurt you and make you bleed. And a broken heart only teaches you how to walk around broken glass pieces, without getting cut by any.

If I got the chance to erase this pain, I wouldn't. Every day I feel a new strength taking its place in my bones. I feel myself growing confident, fearless and independent. I am learning, step by step, that having flaws doesn't mean that I deserve less and I am seeing things more clearly, than I did before. Yes, once in a while, the pain becomes unbearable and I cry in anguish, because I just want it to end. But then I remind myself, that this is the price one has to pay, in order to *grow tougher*, day by day.

Chapter 4

PART I

How **TO LOVE** yourself

A broken heart
is as painful
as a broken bone.
And in the way
a broken bone is fixed
through rest,
care and medicine,
a broken heart, too,
is fixed through
the healing power of self-love

The room is silent, the night is cold. I am standing at the door with my bags packed, when fear grips me, and I am unable to move. *'Why is she not leaving, yet?'* my warriors of strength ask one another.

What if I am too damaged? I ask them. *He ruined so many beautiful parts of me, that I fear, if I step out, nobody will love whatever is left of me. My body is marred with his toxic love. Tell me, who will love me?*

For a while, I hear no reply. I begin to lose the courage I had gathered, and turn around to return...

You will, my warriors reply. *You will love yourself.*

Stand in front of the mirror, naked. Let your eyes linger over your whole body. Find your flaws. Think of everything that makes you feel insecure- every little thing about yourself, that you are afraid to show the world. Stare at it in the mirror, until you fall in love with it. Fall in love with every imperfect nook and corner of your body. Because unless you accept what you are made of, and love it- unless you do that, you won't have the courage to be your self around people, without worrying what they think.

I know you want to hold a grudge. I know you want to hurt them, by screening their call. I know you want to make them jealous, by uploading a picture with someone they dislike, but hear me out, and believe me if you can-

Time will end one day and the only thing you will wish is that instead of acting in ways that would affect someone else, you would've acted in ways that would affect your own self and helped you turn your life around.

Today, if you sit on the footpath wailing your heart out, people will walk around you, to avoid stumbling into your mess. *Times have changed.* You cannot expect someone to pick you up, every time you fall. Besides, you mustn't wait for someone to do what you are supposed to do for yourself. You should simply stand up, scream at the traffic if you want, stomp on the curb, kick the lamp post maybe, and after letting off some steam, you should dust your clothes and march on.

You push loving yourself to another day because you don't think it is important. You have always been the kind of person, who puts others needs before your own, and it has left your heart with very less love to live with. So while it is a great quality to be as giving as you are, you need to remember, that if you give your love away to other people, then you need to pour double that same amount into your own self, every single day.

You often doubt yourself, because you think you are not beautiful. So here are two things to remember- the world's definition of beauty is clichéd, and being different is a rare quality, that you should be proud of. Don't ever forget, that there is something about you that makes you different from everyone else. It lies within you. It is your superpower. It is what your parents proudly tell their friends about. It is what your soulmate will fall in love with. It is what your friends admire about you. So on days when you doubt yourself, remember that although it may not always be in plain sight, there exists within you something so wonderfully beautiful, that it makes the people around you feel blessed, for simply getting a chance to know you.

You long for him, because there is an emptiness in you; a craving for love. So give your heart what it needs. Pour buckets and buckets of love into your heart, to the point that it overflows. Once you, yourself, fill what's empty within you, you no longer live in need of someone else to make you feel complete.

Some days, my flaws grow voices and echo loudly in my mind, till they almost break me. They almost break the courage I have built, to live with my imperfections. On such days, I feel like I might give in and allow my flaws to convince me that I am not beautiful. But it's days like this, that I have to be the strongest on. I have to silence that negative voice in my head and repeatedly tell myself, that my flaws do not ruin my beauty, but simply add to it.

Yes, you are broken. But no, you cannot wait for someone to come along and fix you. You are the only person who can fix you. You knew what you were like, when you were whole. You know where every piece belongs. So tell me, how can you expect someone else to put you together? The people who love you- they can only remind you of the beautiful picture you are trying to build, but you, and only you, can truly recreate it.

You undermine your own ability to be happy. You believe it is a task too difficult to accomplish on your own, and so you pass the responsibility to someone else. But you couldn't be more wrong. You have in you, the power to be anything you want. And just like every other thing in this world, happiness is something that requires effort and hard work. It isn't something you are gifted,

it is something you have to fight for.

I push the dry flowers away, and make way for me to walk through. My jeans are torn and muddy, my hands are cut, and my eyes are tired, but I can't stop. She had been missing for too long now, and I had made a promise to myself. A promise that I would find her, and bring her back. So I cut through whatever came in my way, I climbed walls, I crawled through ditches, and when I finally stepped into the clearing, I saw her. Standing amidst tall trees, a ray of light kissing her skin, through the canopy. I walked up to her and tapped her on the shoulder. When she turned around, I looked myself in the eye.

There you are, I said, *I've been looking for you everywhere.*

One day, you will be sitting in your balcony, sipping hot coffee, while watching rain drops race down the glass windows. In that moment of comfortable silence, you will hear the sound of your inner voice. She will remind you of your beauty, of all the amazing qualities you are made of- and with every little thing she reveals about you, you will fall deeply and fondly in love with your own self.

It took me a lot of time and a lot of strength to fall in love with my brokenness. So if you tell me that you're here to fix me, I will ask you to walk away. It wasn't easy to accept the person I have become, but now that I have, I realise that my broken parts have helped me grow into a better human being. So if you can accept who I am and the ugly past I carry with me, then stay. But if you're here to undo my grief, then I suggest you leave.

She never needed anyone to tell her she was beautiful. She believed, what she thought of herself, was much more important than what others thought of her. And so every morning, she'd look into the mirror and say:
'I am gorgeous.
I am stunning.
I am phenomenal.'

And just like that, she was.

You were a castle, long before careless men marched into your world and destroyed you. Now, the men, they are gone- their footprints remain imprinted on your ground- and so I understand, that loving yourself is not easy. But let me remind you, that before the men came, you were standing tall, all on your own. And you can do it once again. You are strong enough to rise from your ruins and love yourself once more. Just keep reminding yourself, that there is an empty throne within you, waiting, desperately, for you to take back the reigns.

In the same way a bolt of lightning strikes glass to create something extraordinarily beautiful, my pain too, did the same for me. My pain entered my body, searing hot, and it burnt all that was green within me. But learning to turn that burnt garden inside me, into an endless line of roses and sunflowers, has brought out my true beauty.

It has turned me into a masterpiece.

PART II

And how your self should **BE LOVED**

You belong to yourself, before you belong to anyone else. And if the person you're in a relationship with, isn't willing to accept that, then you should leave. You should leave because you are, and always should be,

your first priority.

Love is known, to make us feel lighter. And this isn't because, the presence of love erases our pain, but because the presence of love, makes the pain less burdensome. So when you feel like the relationship you are in, is weighing you down, then you must understand that it isn't love. Love doesn't hold you back from soaring high, instead it helps you untangle yourself from every weight that has kept you on ground, for so long.

I know you look for a person's wounds as soon as they say hello, because you feel the need to heal them. But I think it is time you retire from being the person who gives and gives, without expecting anything in return. Remember, you are to be loved as equally as you love others. So do not talk yourself into the idea, that your love is only meant to be given away, but remind yourself, every day, that your love is also meant to be won and cherished.

I have broken my back, and my heart, trying to build homes with people. And after it all, I have realised one thing: two hearts can't build a home all by themselves. They need to work alongside two minds, too. You see, love isn't only about a rush of adrenaline and the feeling of butterflies in your stomach. Love is much more than that. It requires understanding, patience, honesty and most importantly- a great deal of effort.

We often let peoples choices, change our decisions, and that's not right. Remember, what you want, triumphs over what others want. You have worked hard in chasing the path that'll take you to your dreams. Don't allow someone else to ruin your effort, by running you off course.

People who have been hurt too often, after a while, stop believing in the words 'I love you.' They know how carelessly people throw that phrase around. Such people, they know well enough that love isn't defined by the number of times one says 'I love you', but it is proved by the different ways one says it, *without saying it at all.*

Falling in love with one person, doesn't mean that you have to abandon everything else that makes your life. Your friends, your family, your work, your dreams. Each one of these, is as important as the person you love. And if that person truly loves you, he or she will make sure, you don't ever forget that.

You are not meant to carry the responsibility of this relationship on your frail shoulders, all by yourself. Two people, when in love, should equally contribute to the relationship. They both need to make an equal effort and give each other equal time and attention. So if you feel like you, alone, are doing the job that two people are meant to do together, then I am sorry, but that is not how love works.

Do not waste your time on boys who pour sweet lies into your ears. The ones who talk big, but do nothing. The ones who make promises they never intend to keep. The ones who make you wonder whether you're doing the right thing. Do not waste your time on such boys, because they are here to love you from a distance. And that is not what you deserve. You deserve a love that will envelope you so tightly and completely, that no room will be left for doubt.

If you feel like you cannot see the love you deserve, in the eyes or the actions of the person you're with, then leave. You shouldn't have to wake up every morning, uncertain about whether the person you're in a relationship with, loves you or not. That is a burden, too heavy to carry in your mind. So leave, because you deserve to be with someone who will do all he can in his power, to make sure that you never, not even for a second, feel unloved.

Most people settle with the words 'I love you' because they believe that's all there is to love. But there's more. There is so much more. There are butterflies and goose bumps, good morning messages and 3 am surprise visits. There is adrenaline and adventure, laughter and fireworks. So be patient. Wait for someone who gives you all of that instead of settling for someone who gives you only three simple words.

I realised home wasn't a place or a person. Home was a feeling you felt, when the right people made the right effort, to make a place feel comfortable and warm to you.

That's when you feel at home.

If you hesitate to show him your true self, then that's it. That is the moment, you should pack your bags and run. A relationship doesn't allow you to hide behind a veil. On the contrary, it requires you to strip naked and stand with the door to your heart, wide open. And if he doesn't make you feel safe and secure enough, to let down your guard, then he's not worth having at all.

When you love someone, you fall in love with their heart, their mind, their body, their habits, their vision, their morals, their ambition. So if you find yourself in a relationship, where the other person makes you feel, like you need to give up parts of yourself in order to be loved, then you need to rethink that entire relationship. Because love either happens unbounded or doesn't happen at all.

I mean I've done all that. I've chased after love. I've waited for love. I've sacrificed for love. And it left me exhausted. I was tired of doing so much to make love stay. So I gave up. I told myself, that a love that requires me to constantly prove myself, isn't love at all.

If the person you're in a relationship with, asks you to sacrifice something that you love, as an act to prove how much you love them- you should walk away. Your dreams and your ambitions are on one side, and your love for this person is on the other. There is no correlation between the two. So if the person who claims to love you, doesn't understand the importance of your job, or your dreams, in your life- if they cannot accept the struggle that comes with it- then they are not meant for you.

Time and again, you have to remind him to prove his love for you- and that isn't how it should be. If a person really loves you, and I mean really loves you- you will see it in the little things he does to make you happy.

They will try their best to convince you that the love you deserve doesn't exist. They will tell you, that you are meant to give more than you should receive and that saying the words 'I love you' is enough to prove how a person feels. These people; they want an easier way to love- one that doesn't involve effort, thought and time. They want to be in love, without doing what it takes, to stay in love. Walk away from people who offer you such a lousy love, because the love you always dreamed of- it exists. Wait for it. Don't settle for anything less. You were never meant to be loved by the faint-hearted, darling, so be patient. The love you deserve, it'll come your way, one day.

www.ingramcontent.com/pod-product-compliance
Lightning Source LLC
Chambersburg PA
CBHW011238120626
46549CB00009B/3318